Dear Parent:

Congratulations! Your child is taking the first steps on an exciting journey. The destination? Independent reading!

STEP INTO READING® will help your child get there. The program offers five steps to reading success. Each step includes fun stories and colorful art. There are also Step into Reading Sticker Books, Step into Reading Math Readers, Step into Reading Phonics Readers, Step into Reading Write-In Readers, and Step into Reading Phonics Boxed Sets—a complete literacy program with something to interest every child.

Learning to Read, Step by Step!

Ready to Read   Preschool–Kindergarten
• big type and easy words • rhyme and rhythm • picture clues
For children who know the alphabet and are eager to begin reading.

Reading with Help   Preschool–Grade 1
• basic vocabulary • short sentences • simple stories
For children who recognize familiar words and sound out new words with help.

Reading on Your Own   Grades 1–3
• engaging characters • easy-to-follow plots • popular topics
For children who are ready to read on their own.

Reading Paragraphs   Grades 2–3
• challenging vocabulary • short paragraphs • exciting stories
For newly independent readers who read simple sentences with confidence.

Ready for Chapters   Grades 2–4
• chapters • longer paragraphs • full-color art
For children who want to take the plunge into chapter books but still like colorful pictures.

STEP INTO READING® is designed to give every child a successful reading experience. The grade levels are only guides. Children can progress through the steps at their own speed, developing confidence in their reading, no matter what their grade.

Remember, a lifetime love of reading starts with a single step!

Based in part on *The Cat in the Hat Knows a Lot About That!* TV series (Episode 1) © CITH Productions, Inc. (a subsidiary of Portfolio Entertainment, Inc.), and Red Hat Animation, Ltd. (a subsidiary of Collingwood O'Hare Productions, Ltd.), 2010–2011.

THE CAT IN THE HAT Knows a Lot About That! logo and word mark ™ 2010 Dr. Seuss Enterprises, L.P., Portfolio Entertainment, Inc., and Collingwood O'Hare Productions, Ltd. All rights reserved. The PBS KIDS logo is a registered trademark of PBS. Both are used with permission. All rights reserved.

Broadcast in Canada by Treehouse™. Treehouse™ is a trademark of the Corus® Entertainment Inc. group of companies. All Rights Reserved.

Visit us on the Web!
StepIntoReading.com
Seussville.com
pbskids.org/catinthehat
treehousetv.com

Educators and librarians, for a variety of teaching tools, visit us at
www.randomhouse.com/teachers

Library of Congress Cataloging-in-Publication Data
Rabe, Tish.
Show me the honey / by Tish Rabe ; based on a television script by Ken Cuperus ; illustrated by Christopher Moroney.
   p. cm. — (Step into reading. Step 3)
"Based in part on The Cat in the Hat Knows a Lot About That!"
ISBN 978-0-375-86716-3 (trade) — ISBN 978-0-375-96716-0 (lib. bdg.)
I. Cuperus, Ken. II. Moroney, Christopher. III. Cat in the hat knows a lot about that! (Television program). IV. Title.
PZ8.3.R1145 Sh 2010 [E]—dc22 2009042730

Printed in the United States of America
10 9 8 7 6 5 4 3 2 1

STEP INTO READING®

STEP 3

Show Me the Honey

By Tish Rabe

From a script by Ken Cuperus

Illustrated by Christopher Moroney

Random House 🏠 New York

"This morning," said Nick,

"I'd like honey on toast.

That is the breakfast that

I like the most!"

"Me too," said Sally,

"but I'm sorry to say,

it looks like we're all

out of honey today."

"Sally," Nick said,

"your joke isn't funny.

I can't eat my breakfast

if we're out of honey!"

"Did someone say 'honey'?"
cried the Cat. "What a treat!
It's gloppy and sloppy
and sticky and sweet.
I love it on pancakes,
all fluffy and hot.
Please pour me a bit
of the honey you've got!"

"It's all gone," said Nick.

"Is there some in your hat?"

"Oh dear . . . ," said the Cat.

"No, I do not have that.

But I have something else—

a Special Invitation

to Queen Priscilla Buzzoo's

Dance-All-Day Celebration!

She is queen of the bees

and her parties are great.

But we've got to hurry

or we will be late!"

"There's one problem," said Sally.
"Look here and you'll see—
to go to the party
you must be a bee."

Queen Priscilla Buzzoo's
Dance-All-Day Celebration
Meet at the hive
at a quarter past five.
(Bees only, please.)

11

"Don't worry," the Cat said.

"I know what to do.

This is a job for

Thing One and Thing Two!"

So the two Things ran in and
the Cat asked them, "Please,
do something to make us
fit in with the bees."

In a flash those two Things,
with their usual knack,
striped the kids and the Cat
with yellow and black.

"I can't believe it," said Nick.

"I look just like a bee.

This is something that I

never thought I would see!"

"We're off!" said the Cat.
"We will meet Queen Buzzoo.
We'll meet her and greet her
and dance with her too!
Push the Shrinkmadoodle
if you would, please.
It will shrink us down to
the size of the bees."

17

"We'll fly past the ladybugs
and wave to the birds,
who will sing us some songs
that don't have any words.
We will soar and, what's more,
we will dip and we'll dive
through a hole in a tree
and down into the hive."

19

They got to the party
a few minutes late
and were stopped by two bees
who were guarding the gate.
"Excuse me," one said.
"Where is your invitation
to Queen Priscilla Buzzoo's
Dance-All-Day Celebration?"
"Here it is!" Sally said.
The bees said, "Go in!
The special bee dance
is about to begin!"

"Nick and Sally," the Cat said,
"let me introduce you
    to the queen of the bees,
    Queen Priscilla Buzzoo."
"Hello," said the queen.
"Welcome to my hive.
    My party just started
    at a quarter past five."
"Your Beeness," Nick said,
"I'd like to thank you.
    This is the first party
    of bees I've been to!"

Then they heard buzzing,
and in front of the throne
one worker bee started
to dance all alone!
She zigged and she zagged,
then she wiggled
and waggled.

She slipped and she slid
and she jiggled and jaggled.
She swirled and she twirled
with a buzz and a spin,
and then . . .

. . . more and more bees
began to join in!

Soon all the bees were
dancing and twirling.
Wings and antennae
were swinging and swirling.
Then Sally and Nick
began to dance too.
"Bee-utiful!" cried
Queen Priscilla Buzzoo.

"Watch the bees!" said the Cat.

"And you'll get a surprise—

they aren't just dancing

to get exercise!"

"The first bee that danced,"

Sally said, "let me guess.

She was showing them something."

The Cat cried out, "Yes!"

"Her dance showed something
bees need to survive—
where to find nectar to
bring to the hive.
They get nectar from flowers.
It's sticky and sweet.
They use it to make the
sweet honey they eat."

33

"Her special bee dance
   lets the other bees know
   where to find flowers
   and which way to go."

"Can we help them?" asked Sally.

The Cat said, "Indeed!

We can follow and help them

find nectar they need."

"To the Thinga-ma-jigger!

Get ready to fly.

Hold on to your hats

and we'll take to the sky!"

"Let's go!" said Nick.

"If we hurry, we'll see

how bees make honey.

How hard could it be?"

So they flew with the bees
and slurped nectar from flowers,
then returned to the hive
in a couple of hours.

At the hive they spit nectar
into combs, where it dried.
Soon all of those combs
had sweet honey inside.

"In these combs," the queen said,

"we store honey away."

"This is fun!" Sally cried.

"I could do this all day."

42

"Next, we must cover
  the combs," said the queen.
"This protects the honey
  and helps keep it clean."
"I like honey," said Nick.
"I like honey a lot.
  But making it is much
  more work than I thought!"

"It's late," said the Cat,

"and it's time we must go,

but we'll come back to visit

you all soon, I know."

"So long!" buzzed the bees.

"And be sure to come back

anytime you want honey

to eat for a snack."

Back home they all opened
their gifts from the queen—
more jars of honey than
they'd ever seen!
"The note says," said Sally,
"'We want to give you
the world's sweetest honey,
from the Hive of Buzzoo.'"

"I liked meeting the queen
and flying through trees.
But what I liked most,"
Nick said . . .

"... was dancing with bees!"